Musings of the heart

Janeen Fearon

BookLeaf Publishing

Presentation by *BookLeaf Publishing*

Web: www.bookleafpub.com

E-mail: info@bookleafpub.com

ISBN: 9789357215640

First edition 2022

This book is dedicated to those who have loved and those who have lost.

My sincere advice to you is that there is no such thing as a perfect relationship, however there is a relationship out there that would be perfect for you.

ACKNOWLEDGEMENT

I would like to acknowledge God as my source, as He has gifted me with the passion and ability to write. I have truly found peace and solace over the years in expressing my deepest thoughts and feelings, through the creative medium of writing.

I admire great writers and poets such as Maya Angelou and Toni Morrison and I desire to share my message with the world in the same articulate and authentic manner that they did.

PREFACE

Musings of the heart was written to awaken your desire for love and to take you on a imaginative journey.

You will be transported through time and space and will have the opportunity to experience the highs and lows of love, connection, and companionship through the writer's gaze.

Musings of heart is honest, raw and unapologetic, so sit back and enjoy the ride!

LESSONS IN LOVE

You were my muse. You were my love.
You taught me lessons… in love.

You showed me hope and fueled my inner desires.

You set my heart ablaze and helped me to lose inhibitions.

You stirred me, moved me, healed me and for that I am ever grateful.
You helped me to be free.

You taught me so much about love, loss and misguided desires, that do not align with destiny's plan.

You broke me and built me by stretching me to capacity.

You pushed me to be honest with myself and face very hard truths.

You challenged my ideologies, forcing me to make a decision.

I appreciate you for the part that you played in my growth, development and awakening.

I will never regret the lessons that you taught me… in love.

SYNCHRONICITY

We have undeniable synchronicity.

Our goals, our passions and our desires are aligned.

Our mindsets, and our language, our hopes and dreams are in sync.

We are each other's equal, both unique in our experiences and perspectives.

I love our synchronicity even in our idiosyncrasies.

THE COLDEST WINTER

The seasons have changed once again, and I am left with a chill.

The coldness of winter kisses my lips, and the grey sky of loneliness greets me.

The memories of our love play on repeat in the corridors of my mind.

I sigh as I think of the broken promises, the children we talked about, and the places we vowed to visit.

I think on your inconsistencies and the constant uncertainty of a future together.

I could no longer carry the relationship, resuscitating it whenever it slipped into a state of unconsciousness.

You were not ready to embark on a journey with me, and you lacked the maturity and the tools to build.

I realise now that you were never my soul mate, my rock, or my best friend but you were just my coldest winter.

You have taught me to wrap up warm and to ensure I have a map, as I may have to travel alone.

ODE TO HUNTER

Hunter...I see you undressing me with your eyes.

You consider me prey and are excited at the prospect of a chase.

Although coy at times, I am nobody's fool, and I will not succumb to your advances.

I will be polite and take my leave at exactly the right moment.

You see, I am not impressed with your bravado, your accolades, or your wealth.

I understand that for you this is merely a game and I choose not to engage.

Farewell hunter... as this is an unsuccessful pursuit because I know better than to dalliance with a handsome stranger.

CLOSER

I desire to be closer to you.

Closer to you and wrapped around you like a blanket.

Closer to you and circling you like the earth orbits the sun.

Closer to you because I am enthralled and enamoured with you.

Closer to you, sharing intimate thoughts.

Closer to you by working through life's difficult situations.

Can we get closer?

OVERFLOW

I am living in the overflow of your love.

I am sustained by your breath, your touch, and your kiss.

Your words are like water running deep within the core of my being, cleansing my inner parts, and quenching my thirst.

I drink of your fountain daily and bask in the overflow of your love.

HEALING

I have been healing, dancing, and painting.

I have been growing, feeding on what nourishes my soul and cultivating healthy habits.

I have been investing in myself and investing in my future.

I have been sowing seeds of love, and I have been giving hope to all that I meet.

I have been underpinning faulty foundations and breaking up the fallow ground.

I have been upgrading and seeking more wisdom and insight.

No more past trauma, old mindsets, and phycological regrets. No more old stories or limiting beliefs.

This version of me that you see is currently under construction, and I am actively seeking out my healing.

SUDDENLY

We once experienced true love in its purest and rarest form.

Young love untainted and full of endless possibilities.

You made me laugh as we talked for hours. You listened to me and for the first time I felt seen, significant and safe.

We wrote poetry together and created songs, as you brought out my hidden gifts and talents.

You covered me and showed what real connection feels like and I will never forget the time we shared.

You came into my life suddenly and left at the same rate, but your impact will be with me for an eternity and our song will forever remain.

QUESTIONS

"Honey… how are you going to reach me?"

"Are you more than willing to teach me?"

"How are you going to love me, comfort and put no one above me?"

"How are you going to care for me, cherish and be there for me?"

"Do you really admire me, and how can you inspire me?"

"Will you make time for me, and would you really walk the line for me?"

These are my questions!

RECIPROCITY

The ebb and flow between interdependent entities.

The giving and receiving of love.

Knowing that you will experience true mutuality, nothing hidden or held back.

The feeling of harmony, this is true reciprocity.

MUSINGS OF THE HEART

Straight to the heart of me.

Pulling me undone, lowering my guard.

Weakening my defences and causing me to retreat.

I am unravelling and falling, as your tipped arrow has pierced the very centre of my heart.

SACRED NIGHT

Our night will be full of euphoric bliss.
The meeting of two minds, two hearts, and two souls.
Our destinies intertwined, and our hopes and dreams aligned.

Nothing will compare to our sacred night.

All our secrets are revealed in a space of welcomed vulnerability.
Our passions are unleashed and untamed with the forsaking of all our insecurities.

Nothing will compare to our sacred night.

Experiencing intimacy that transcends space and time.
Knowing you deeply and becoming yours wholeheartedly, truly understanding the meaning of becoming one.

Nothing can compare to our sacred night.

LIFE

Whispers, sweet kisses blown.
Keys in the door, “honey, I’m home.”
Proud of our legacy look how they’ve grown.
Nursery, school, college and now they’ve left home.
Holidays away having fun in the sun.
Look how we’ve changed you’re “Dad” and I’m “Mum”.
Retired early so we can relax, to focus on each other and live life to the max.

FLEETING MOMENT

You move slowly and carefully to avoid being heard or detected.

Laying low, waiting for an opportune moment to pounce.

Looking for an opening and hoping for a hint of latent vulnerability.

I am aware of your intent.

We once had a moment but nothing more will ever come of that.

You are a thought of the past and hold no weight in my present or future.

You were just a fleeting moment, nothing to be considered.

OUR WORDS ARE OUR WORLD

The words we speak create life or death.

Let us speak love and peace over our relationship.

I see you as a man who is full of greatness and power and who can achieve all things.

In turn see my faithfulness, and my ability to nurture and speak life into my motherhood and caregiving.

Let us create something beautiful with our words because our words become our world.

WORTH THE WAIT

Waiting for your emergence and the day of your reveal.

Robed in royal regalia to welcome my king into the palace.

Your sceptre and crown are positioned by your throne.

Singing as you enter in, you were worth the wait.

HIDE AND SEEK

Where are you, my love?

I have searched over hilltops high and mountain peaks.

I have looked for you in valleys low and forest glades. Yet I still cannot find you.

Please uncover yourself and relieve me of this search.

For I am tired and worn and need your arms as a refuge.

Come to me, my love, and let us retire from playing hide and seek.

LEGACY

I thank God that you have finally arrived...

Today is a day that we have been waiting for in earnest expectation.

You are truly beautiful and perfect in everyway.

Many months of prayer and travail have brought you forth.

You are the embodiment of every good part of us and we vow to keep you safe.

You are a dream come true and you are our legacy.

www.ingramcontent.com/pod-product-compliance
Lightning Source LLC
Chambersburg PA
CBHW051717130826
49812CB00034B/1232
9789357215640